BIRDS
FEET & LEGS

BIRDS
FEET & LEGS

Jack B. Kochan

STACKPOLE
BOOKS

Published by
STACKPOLE BOOKS
5067 Ritter Road
Mechanicsburg, PA 17055

Printed in the United States of America

10 9 8 7 6 5 4 3 2 1

First edition

Cover design by Caroline Miller

Library of Congress Cataloging-in-Publication Data

Kochan, Jack
    Birds—feet & legs / Jack Kochan. — 1st ed.
       p.   cm.
    Includes bibliographical references.
    ISBN 0-8117-2515-4
    1. Wood-carving.   2. Birds in art.   3. Birds—Anatomy.   I. Title.
    II. Title: Birds—feet & legs.
TT199.7.K63   1994
731'.832—dc20
                                                    93-48096
                                                      CIP

*To Peter, without whose encouragement, inspiration, and friendship
this book would never have been started*

Contents

Preface

For many years I have watched wild-fowl carvers, both beginning and experienced, produce good quality work that just was not blue-ribbon material. Each year these carvers enter shows only to leave, once again, unrecognized for their many hours of effort to produce life-like replicas of nature's feathered creatures.

I'm sure they have all asked themselves, "Why? What am I doing wrong?" Asking themselves won't get the answer. They must ask the master carvers, the world-class champions. Even then, they may not learn what is absent from their work that allows it to pass the eyes of show judges without a second glance. Most likely they are making the same mistakes again and again because no one really tells them what they need to know.

I, too, was caught in this frustrating stalemate until an artist friend said that I could not accurately draw or sculpt the outside until I knew what the inside looked like. This simple statement says it all. An architect can't design a skyscraper without knowing how the steel framework goes together.

Even if you don't plan to enter your carving in competition, you still want to make it as realistic as possible. You will be able to sculpt a more lifelike bird by knowing and understanding what is underneath the feathers.

Knowing the anatomy of your subject, be it bird or animal, will serve to increase the accuracy and realism of the carving. Many times when talking to beginning or even advanced carvers, I find that they do not understand the terminology used to describe a bird or a part of a bird. This simple study of bird anatomy should be helpful in producing a more accurate carving and help you to better understand what the master carvers are saying when they answer your questions.

Each book in this series is devoted to

one part of a bird's anatomy and also includes much about the physiology and habits of different species. Anatomy by itself is only one small portion of ornithology. I have tried to include as much other pertinent information as possible in order that you may better understand the "why's and how's" related to the anatomical structure. The information contained in this book has been compiled from personal research and many sources of reference.

The objective of this book is to help carvers and artists at all levels of proficiency obtain a better understanding of the structure of a bird. This knowledge, I hope, will help them improve their work. It will be a very rewarding feeling to think that every carver or artist who reads this book will have learned at least one important thing from it.

This book was written specifically with the carver or artist in mind, but it contains sufficient technical information so that it could be used as a reference primer for the budding ornithologist as well.

ONE

History of Birds

Knowing what prehistoric birds looked like is probably not of much use to the artist, but an understanding of how birds have evolved provides a foundation for additional studies of birds. The carver or artist must learn more than just what a bird looks like. There must be an understanding of the bird's habits, habitat, and peculiarities in order to depict it accurately. Just like the architect, whose skyscraper is not designed without taking into consideration where it will be located and how it will be landscaped, the artist must also consider all that surrounds the species being portrayed.

You would not depict a grouse, for example, with a mouse in its claws, or a loon perched on a rocky cliff. Knowing the habits of the species is just as important as knowing the species, and many times the artist or carver will spend at least as much time researching the habits and habitat as researching the species itself.

In 1861, a worker at a limestone quarry in Bavaria discovered the fossil remains of a feather. That same year at another limestone quarry, an incomplete fossil skeleton of the same kind of bird was unearthed. This bird, named Archeopteryx, is estimated to have lived about 140–150 million years ago (Jurassic period), and is presently the oldest known bird ever recorded.

Other fossils found in France show evidence of a gooselike bird, the size of an ostrich, that lived about 125 million years ago (Cretaceous period). In North America, fossil remains of a snipelike bird were discovered in New Jersey in 1834, and later, in the 1870s, other remains were found in Maryland, Idaho, Kansas, North Carolina, and New Mexico. In 1876, a fossil bone was uncovered in New Mexico that was about 50 million years old. This bone was from a rather strange, seven-foot-tall, flightless bird similar to the ostrich, with a head size comparable to that of a horse.

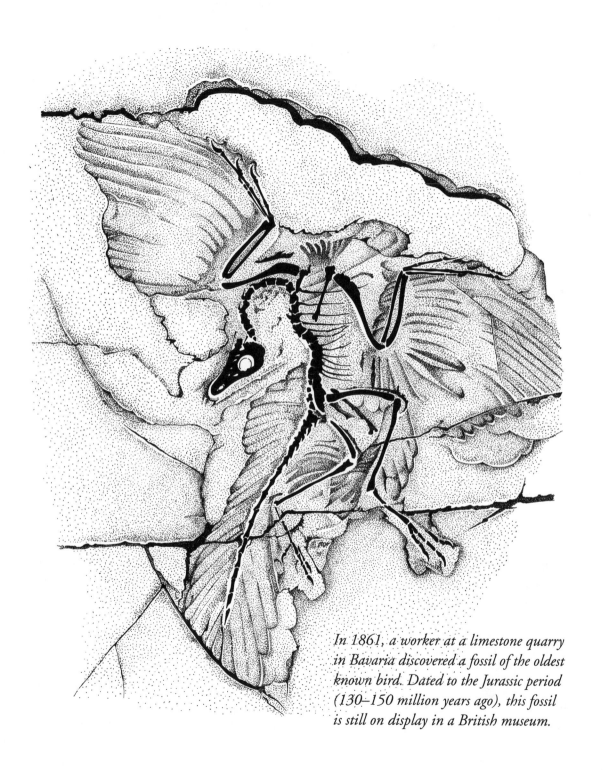

In 1861, a worker at a limestone quarry in Bavaria discovered a fossil of the oldest known bird. Dated to the Jurassic period (130–150 million years ago), this fossil is still on display in a British museum.

Compared with other animals, very little is known about prehistoric birds. Paleontologists (those who study fossils) have been able to piece together a relatively accurate description of these ancient birds by using their knowledge of present-day birds and incorporating logical assumptions.

Archeopteryx was a bird with a long lizardlike, totally feathered tail, and a bill that had teeth in the upper and lower jaws. The wings each had three fingerlike projections with claws that were probably used to cling to trees or to catch prey. The lizardlike skeletal features were very similar to certain known dinosaurs, and other features indicate that this bird probably was not a good flyer.

Although Archeopteryx was not a bird as we know birds today, it definitely was not a reptile because it had feathers. About the size of a large pigeon, this ancient bird was probably a gliding flyer rather than a flapping wing flyer. It had strong legs and most likely ran or hopped on the ground most of the time, or perhaps hopped or glided from tree branch to tree branch.

There is much that can be learned about a bird by studying its anatomy, and there is still very much remaining to be learned. Man has always been fascinated by, fearful of, or spiritually drawn to birds. Ancient Greeks, who named the owl, compared this bird to Athena, the goddess of wisdom; thus, "wise as an owl" is still a well-known phrase. Early Romans considered it a bad omen if the "sacred chicken" would not eat before a pending battle. Drawings on the walls of caves by early man suggest that humans have always been attracted to birds, perhaps because of their fascination with or desire for flight.

As recently as the last decade or two, certain tribes of people on South Pacific islands used the feathers of the honeyeater bird as a form of money. Many tribes of American Indians used bird feathers as part of their dress and believed they were spiritually joined to certain species.

From Archeopteryx to the modern, birds have evolved, changed, and adapted to their needs. Many species are now extinct, and people have only recently become more aware of the ecological damages being done to further the extinction list. In 1681, the dodo of Mauritius Island in the Indian Ocean was the first recorded species of bird to become extinct at the hands of humans. Fortunately, people are becoming better informed about environmental conditions that cause catastrophic changes. The wildfowl artist plays an important role in educating people about these conditions, and the more the artist knows about birds, the better he or she can depict these conditions. Anatomy is one way to learn more about our feathered creatures.

Archeopteryx was a rather strange looking bird with three fingerlike claws on each wing, sharp teeth in its mouth, and a fully feathered, long, lizardlike tail. Slightly larger than the common pigeon, Archeopteryx probably was a gliding type of flyer because it had no sternal keel that would indicate a large, strong breast.

TABLE I
Geological Time Table

PERIOD	EPOCH	MILLIONS OF YEARS OLD
QUATERNARY	Recent	.01
	Pleistocene	1.5–3.5
TERTIARY	Pliocene	7
	Miocene	26
	Oligocene	37–38
	Eocene	53–54
	Paleocene	65
CRETACEOUS	Late	100
	Early	136
JURASSIC	Late	155
	Middle	170
	Early	180–190
TRIASSIC		230

TWO

Topography

In order to understand the terminology in the following text, you should become familiar with the general areas of a bird, or what is often referred to as topography. In ornithology, topography is the mapping and naming of the surface areas of a bird. This gives a precise means of describing a segment, part, or location, using common terminology that everyone understands. If, for example, you talk about the nape, then others who understand topography will immediately know to what part of the bird you are referring. Some other locating terms used by ornithologists are proximal, distal, dorsal, ventral, anterior, and posterior.

Proximal refers to the point closest to the centerline of the body or the innermost point, whereas distal is just the opposite or the farthest point from the body centerline. Dorsal refers to the top or uppermost part and ventral refers to the bottom, lower, or under part. Anterior refers to the front or frontal part while posterior is the opposite and refers to the rear or hind part. The ability to communicate well is reason enough to become familiar with the parts of a bird.

The drawing below is not of any particular species; it is merely a road map of a bird in general. Each of these areas will be covered in detail in later books.

The scientific study of the surface structure, shape, and external characteristics of a bird or animal is called morphology, which also includes the study of some of the internal characteristics. Anatomy is the scientific study of the internal structure, systems, and organs of a bird or animal. This includes the skeleton and the nervous, muscular, circulatory, and other systems, which are usually studied by dissecting the specimen. Topography divides a bird, or any animal, into defined sections and names these sections for identification.

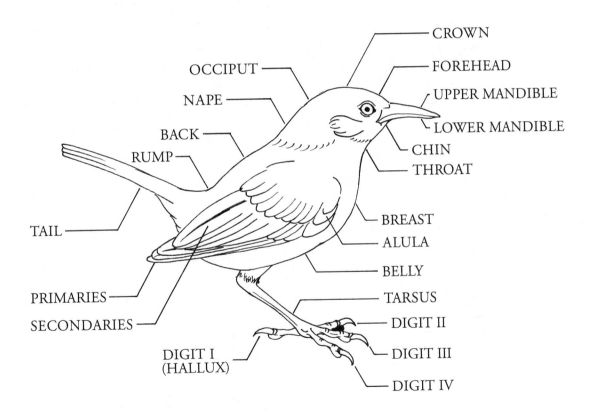

Not of any particular species, this illustration shows the significant areas of the topography of a bird.

The leg of a bird can be divided into three main segments: (1) the femoral segment or thigh, (2) the crus segment or drumstick, and (3) the tarsus and toes or foot. The thigh and crus form the leg, and the tarsus and toes make up the foot. The toes are identified by Roman numerals with the hallux being toe number I.

Each section of topography has definite boundaries. The femoral segment begins at the proximal (closest to the body) end of the femur where it attaches to the pelvis and extends to the knee. The crus is the area from the knee joint to the ankle joint or heel. The tarsus or shank is the upper part of the foot and is the area from the ankle joint to the point of attachment of the toes. The toes are called digits, and are the distal (outermost) extremities of the foot that are terminated in long, sharp claws.

The outward appearance of the leg has great diversity between species, and these differences usually correspond to the varied habits of different species. Wading birds, for example, generally have long stiltlike legs while perching birds normally have much shorter legs.

The feet of most aquatic birds have a fleshy webbing between the toes and are said to be palmate. Some have fleshy lobes on either side of the toes—as on a grebe—and are said to be lobate. There are about nine thousand different species of birds cataloged today, and there are just as many variations of legs and feet.

The topography of the leg is divided into three main sections: the femoral segment, the crus, and the foot. The toes are called digits and are referred to by number.

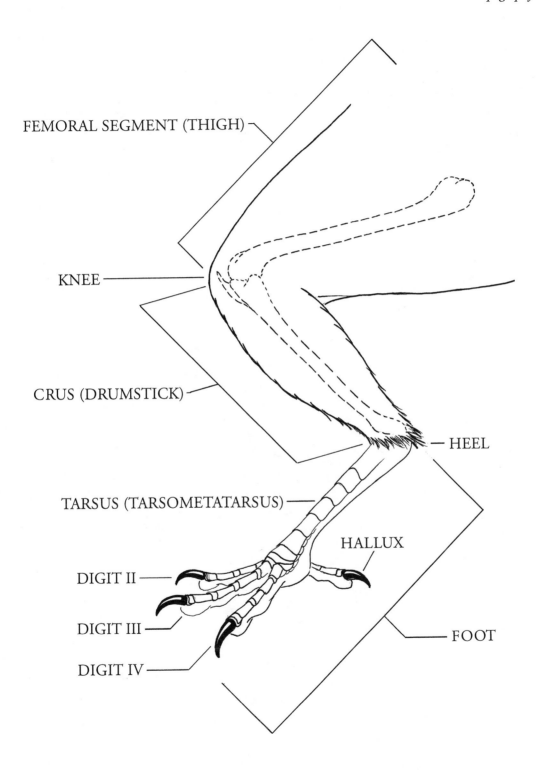

FEMORAL SEGMENT (THIGH)

KNEE

CRUS (DRUMSTICK)

HEEL

TARSUS (TARSOMETATARSUS)

HALLUX

DIGIT II

DIGIT III

DIGIT IV

FOOT

THREE

Skeletal Structure

A bird's feet are perhaps the most difficult part of the anatomy to accurately reproduce in a carving. There is such a variety of techniques in use today, and so many books available describing them, that no attempt will be made here to select any single method. It is more important that you learn and understand how the leg and foot are constructed.

The skeleto-muscular system of a bird is the mechanical structure and motor mechanism that allows it to move from place to place by walking or flying. The scientific study of bones and the skeletal systems of birds or other animals is called osteology.

Bones that make up the skeleton in birds are uniquely different from other vertebrates in that they have a spongelike interior containing many air pockets. This makes them very lightweight, yet strong. Bone is a living tissue that can adapt to changes and repair itself. Before the breeding season, the females of some species store calcium in their bones, which is later used for making eggshells.

The point where two or more bones meet is known as a joint. There are two types of joints. When two bones meet but do not move with respect to each other, this is called a suture, whereas a movable joint is said to be articulated. Most articulated joints are enclosed in a fluid-filled cavity and are called synovial joints. The synovial fluid at the joint is the lubrication for the moving bone parts and is kept in place with a fibrous tissue that encapsulates the entire joint.

The bones are held together at the joints with ligaments, which are attached to the adjoining bones of a joint. Ligaments act like ropes, which have strength against a pulling force but collapse when they are pushed on. Most joints are movable, but not all joints will articulate, or move, in the same manner.

The shape of the bones at the joint helps to determine the direction, and somewhat the extent, of movement at that joint. The dorsal (upper) end of the femur, for example, is a somewhat rounded shape that fits into a pocket formed by the bones of the pelvic girdle. The pocket of this "ball-and-socket" joint is called the acetabulum and allows the femur to rotate and move in a slightly cone-shaped arc around it.

The skeletal structure of a bird's leg is homologous—or similar in structure—to that of a human. What is normally thought of as the leg of a bird is, in reality, the upper part of the foot. The leg is usually heavily muscled and hidden beneath the flank feathers so that it is not seen. What most people call the leg is actually the tarsus or the upper part of the foot.

Regardless of how the leg and foot appear on the surface, the skeletal structure is basically the same on all species. The upper part of the leg (thigh) contains the femur, which joins, at the proximal (closest to the body) end, to the pelvic girdle. Below the femur are two bones that lie parallel to each other. The larger of the two is the tibiotarsus, or simply the tibia, and the smaller of the two bones is the fibula.

Where the dorsal ends of the tibiotarsus and fibula join the femur is the knee. The knee joint is somewhat saddle-shaped, which allows only for longitudinal movement and greatly restricts lateral (side-to-side) movement. The knee bends forward as in man. The dorsal end of the tibiotarsus, on the anterior (frontal) side, is slightly enlarged and protruding. This enlargement is called the cnemial crest.

The skeleton of a bird's leg can be compared to that of a human. In a bird, some of the metatarsals have fused together to form the tarsometatarsus. This bone is sometimes called the cannon bone, since its shape resembles the barrel of a gun.

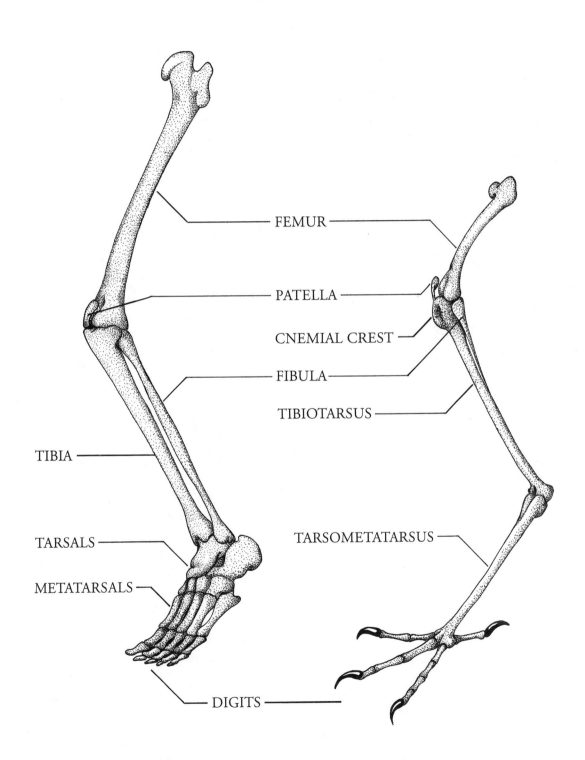

FEMUR

PATELLA

CNEMIAL CREST

FIBULA

TIBIOTARSUS

TIBIA

TARSALS

METATARSALS

TARSOMETATARSUS

DIGITS

The patella, or kneecap, is a small bone above the cnemial crest at the front of the knee. Sometimes the patella is merely a flattened extension of the cnemial crest, and in some species it does not exist at all. Grebes, however, have both a large patella and an extension of the cnemial crest.

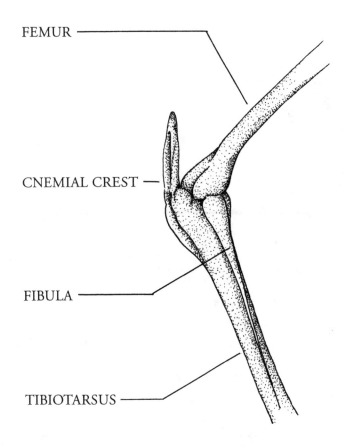

FEMUR ——————

CNEMIAL CREST —

FIBULA ——————

TIBIOTARSUS ——————

The patella does not appear on all species and sometimes is just a flattened extension of the cnemial crest. A few species have both a cnemial crest and a patella.

The lower end of the fibula is joined to the tibiotarsus with ligaments to form the ankle. The fibula is much smaller in diameter than the tibiotarsus, and its lower end, usually splinter-shaped, does not extend the full length of the tibiotarsus. This lower section of the leg is the crus. The crus segment is more commonly known as the "drumstick." The remaining skeletal structure below the crus makes up the foot of the bird.

The foot can be divided into two sections. The upper section of the foot contains the tarsometatarsus, but is generally called the metatarsus, or more commonly just the tarsus or the shank. Because this is normally the part that is visible, many people think it is the leg of the bird and mistake the heel for the knee. This also leads them to believe that a bird's knee bends backward, which is not the case.

Even in ornithology this misnomer is implied by having a group of birds labeled the "thick knee" family (Burhinidae). Birds in this family were so named because of their rather large knee, which is actually their heel, and include species such as the double-striped thick knee. At the dorsal (upper) end of the tarsus on the posterior (rearward) side is the heel.

When comparing a bird's foot skeleton to that of a human, you will notice that in birds, some bones have disappeared while others have fused together. Three metatarsals have fused to form the tarsus with a tripod structure at the distal end for the attachment of the forward toes. This bone of the tarsus is sometimes called the cannon bone because of its resemblance to the barrel of a gun. A prominent metatarsal is connected by ligaments at the posterior (rear) and somewhat inboard to the tarsus for the attachment of the hallux.

On the rear of the tarsus, at the dorsal end, is a double-ridge projection called the hypotarsus. The hypotarsus is a guide for the Achilles tendon, which is described in the chapter about muscles.

The toes, or digits, make up the lower part of the foot. Unlike humans, most birds have from two to four toes. The typical perching bird has four toes; an ostrich has only two. The toe normally projecting to the rear is called the hallux. It is comparable to the human "big toe." The three toes projecting forward are identified simply by number (toe numbers II, III, and IV), with number II being the innermost toe and the hallux being toe number I. Toes are referred to as digits, and this numbering system, using Roman numerals, is known as the digital formula.

The phalanges are the bones that make up the toes, and the outermost phalanx—singular—of each toe has a horny extension creating a strong curved claw. The hallux has two phalanges and is often much smaller than the other toes and, in some cases, is totally absent. On many species of waterfowl, the hallux is very small with little more than the claw exposed.

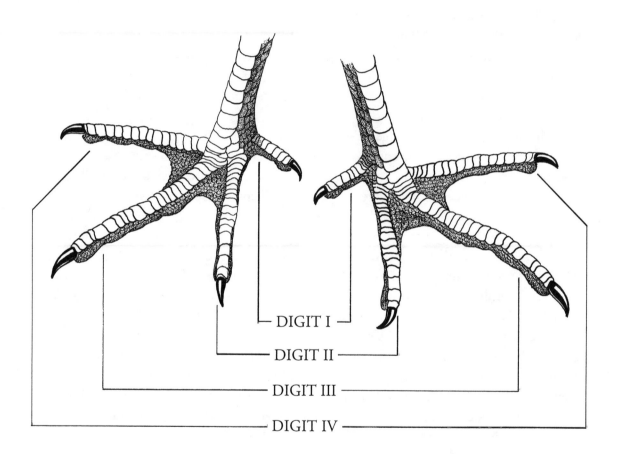

DIGIT I

DIGIT II

DIGIT III

DIGIT IV

The numbering system of the toes is called the digital formula, with the hallux always being toe number I, and the innermost toe being number II. Each toe contains one more phalanx than its digital number.

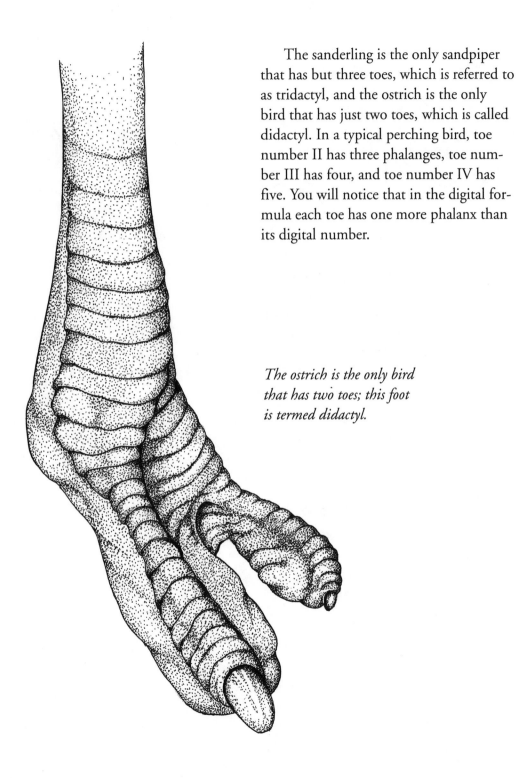

The sanderling is the only sandpiper that has but three toes, which is referred to as tridactyl, and the ostrich is the only bird that has just two toes, which is called didactyl. In a typical perching bird, toe number II has three phalanges, toe number III has four, and toe number IV has five. You will notice that in the digital formula each toe has one more phalanx than its digital number.

The ostrich is the only bird that has two toes; this foot is termed didactyl.

The most common arrangement of toe position is three toes forward and one toe (hallux) to the rear. On some birds, such as the woodpecker, toe number IV is more often seen pointing to the rear rather than forward, and on others such as the swift, all four toes may point forward.

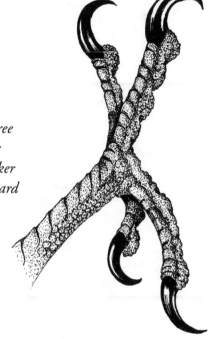

The most common arrangement is three toes pointing forward with the hallux pointing to the rear, but the woodpecker normally has two toes pointing rearward and two toes pointing forward.

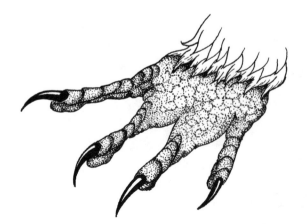

The swift has the uncommon arrangement of all four toes pointing forward.

The legs of all birds have the same basic skeletal structure. The variations would be the length and diameter of the various bones and the number of toes. A heron, for example, has an unusually long tarsus and tibiotarsus, which makes its legs well adapted for wading in search of food.

The long legs of the heron are well suited for wading in shallow water in search of food.

FOUR

Surface Appearance

The feet of birds are categorized, by ornithologists, into three characteristic groups: (1) by characteristics of the tarsus, (2) by the characteristics of the toes, and (3) by characteristics of the claws. The tarsus is generally classed into seven different types, the toes by ten different types, and the claws by five different types. The toe positions, surface texture, and claw shapes are quite important if you want an accurately made carving and, as you can see, there can be many variations.

The characteristics of the tarsus have several different cross-sectional shapes in different species. The most common shape is the "rounded in front" and in ornithology is labeled as acutiplantar. The sides are somewhat flattened and converge to a rather sharp ridge at the rear. This is the cross-sectional shape of nearly all perching species.

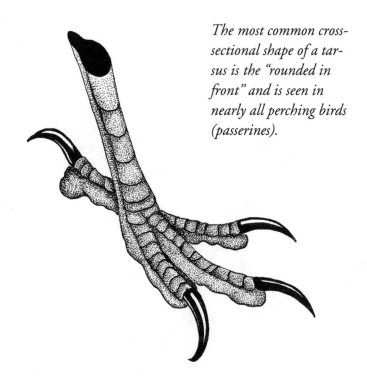

The most common cross-sectional shape of a tarsus is the "rounded in front" and is seen in nearly all perching birds (passerines).

Occasionally, the tarsus is "rounded in front and behind," as in the horned lark, and is labeled latiplantar. In a few species, the tarsus is very flat side-to-side with sharp edges front and rear, as in loons and a few other aquatic birds. This tarsus is said to be compressed, and provides a streamlined shape when the birds are swimming.

The compressed tarsus is flattened side to side with sharp ridges front and back, as in loons.

Sometimes the tarsus is "rounded in front and behind," as in the horned lark.

The tarsus is usually covered with a horny skin called the podotheca, or tarsal sheath, which extends to the tips of the toes. The part of the podotheca that covers the front of the tarsus is called the acrotarsium, while the posterior covering is called the planta.

The surface appearance of the tarsus is categorized into seven different types. Unless it is feathered, as in some hawks and owls, the texture on the surface of the podotheca is often cut up into overlapping, horny scales called scutella, and is said to be scutellate, as in the grosbeak, finch, or sparrow. (The word "scutellum," singular, is taken from Latin, meaning "little shield.")

When the tarsal sheath is divided into overlapping horny plates, as in the crow, it is said to be scutellate.

The scutella are normally arranged in a definite pattern and often overlap like shingles. They are usually found on the acrotarsium (front side of the tarsus) and almost always on the top of the toes.

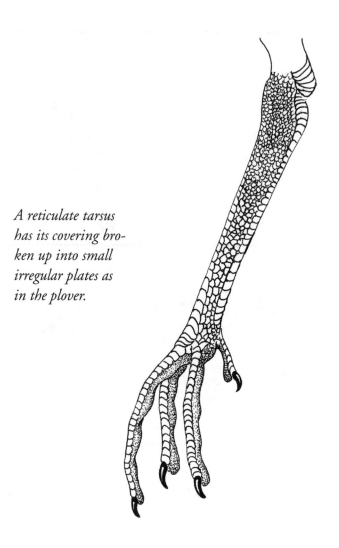

A reticulate tarsus has its covering broken up into small irregular plates as in the plover.

When the tarsus is textured with
small, irregular plates, as in the plover, it is
said to be reticulate. Some birds, like the
pigeon, have a tarsus that is scutellate in
front and reticulate behind, and are
classed as scutellate-reticulate.

*The common pigeon
has a tarsus that is
scutellate in front and
reticulate in back.*

A booted or ocreate tarsus is mostly smooth in front and back without any scales or plates, except in some cases at the extreme lower end, and is called holothe-cal. When the tarsus is scutellate in front and smooth on the plantar (rear) surface, it is said to be scutellate-booted, as in the gray catbird.

Sometimes the scutella (horny plates) of the tarsus have serrated edges, as found on the planta (posterior surface of the tarsus) of a grebe, and are said to be serrate.

A tarsus that is smooth in front and back is said to be booted. Sometimes a booted tarsus is scutellate at the extreme lower end.

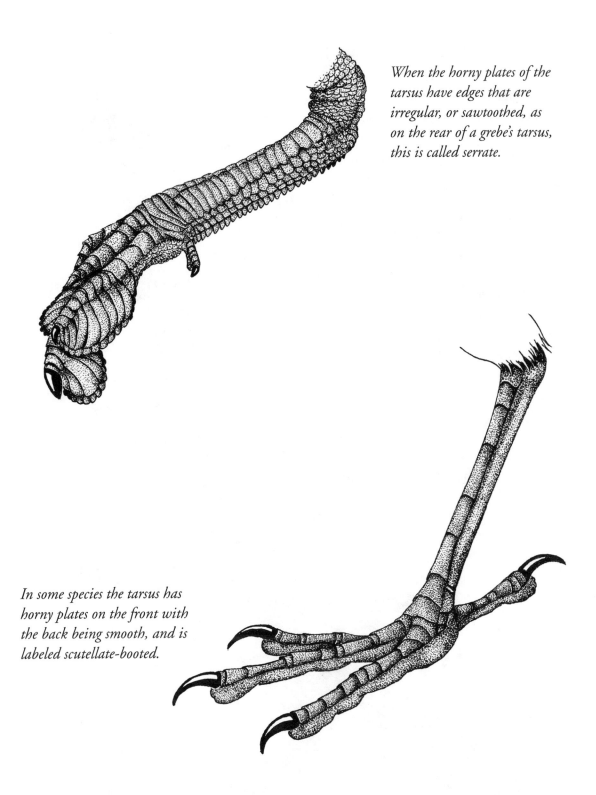

When the horny plates of the tarsus have edges that are irregular, or sawtoothed, as on the rear of a grebe's tarsus, this is called serrate.

In some species the tarsus has horny plates on the front with the back being smooth, and is labeled scutellate-booted.

Occasionally, as in the ring-necked pheasant, the back of the tarsus is peculiarly modified to form a spur and is said to be spurred.

Spurs grow at the inner rear of the tarsus and are outgrowths of the bone that are covered with a hard podotheca (horny sheath). An adult male wild turkey has a spur, about an inch in length, which is sharply pointed and curved upward. This spurred foot is used to fight rivals during the spring mating season. The jungle fowl has an extremely long spur used for the same purpose, and it is not unusual for one of the birds to be killed during the fight. Normally, only the male of the species will develop spurs.

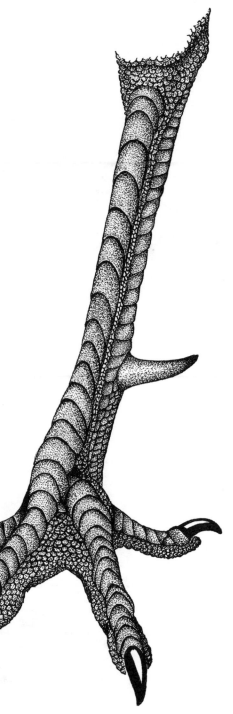

A spur is a horny outgrowth of the tarsus. The male wild turkey has a spur about an inch in length and curved upward. This spurred tarsus becomes a defensive weapon during the mating season.

In all birds, the front toes are joined to the tarsometatarsus at the same level, but the hind toe or hallux varies in position. When the hallux is joined to the tarsus at the same level as the other toes, it is said to be incumbent, as in the meadowlark.

Sometimes the hallux is joined to the tarsus at a much higher level than the other toes and is said to be elevated. In some cases the hallux is joined so high on the tarsus that its claw barely touches the ground, as in the ring-necked pheasant.

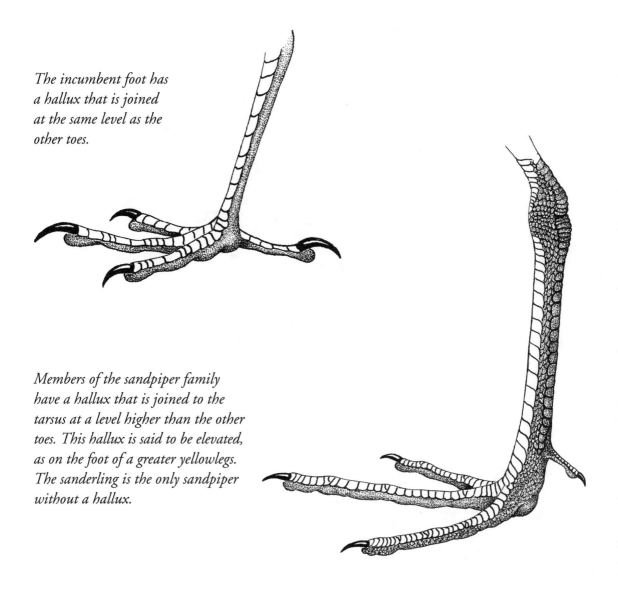

The incumbent foot has a hallux that is joined at the same level as the other toes.

Members of the sandpiper family have a hallux that is joined to the tarsus at a level higher than the other toes. This hallux is said to be elevated, as on the foot of a greater yellowlegs. The sanderling is the only sandpiper without a hallux.

The position or arrangement of the toes, or the particular specialized function of a foot, is further categorized into ten types. Each type could have some variation.

Anisodactyl. This is the most common arrangement where the hallux is to the rear and the other three toes are in front, as seen in most perching birds.

Syndactyl. Toe numbers III and IV (middle and outer) are united for most of their length and share a broad sole as in the belted kingfisher.

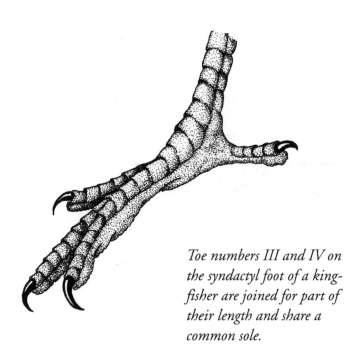

Toe numbers III and IV on the syndactyl foot of a kingfisher are joined for part of their length and share a common sole.

Zygodactyl. In this arrangement the toes are paired, with toe numbers II and III (inner and middle) in front and toe number IV and hallux to the rear, as in a woodpecker or cuckoo.

The zygodactyl foot has the toes paired with toe numbers II and III in front and number IV and hallux to the rear, as in a cuckoo.

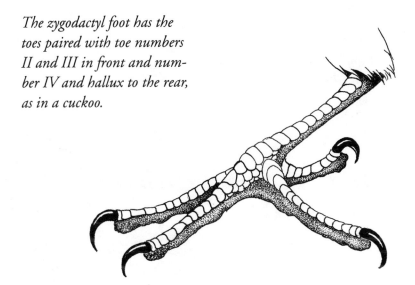

Heterodactyl. The toes are paired with toe number III and number IV in front, and toe number II and hallux to the rear, as in a trogon.

Pamprodactyl. This somewhat unusual arrangement has all four toes turned forward, as in the swift.

A swift's foot is pamprodactyl, with all four toes pointing forward.

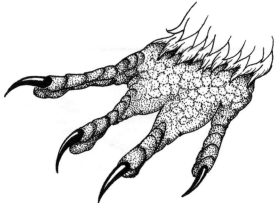

Raptorial. The toes are heavily padded on the bottom with large, strong, curved claws (talons) as in hawks, owls, or eagles.

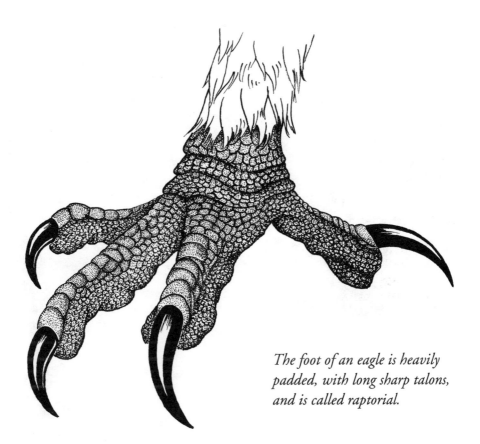

The foot of an eagle is heavily padded, with long sharp talons, and is called raptorial.

Palmate. Quite common on ducks, geese, and gulls, where the three forward toes are joined for their entire length by a fleshy web.

Semipalmate. The toes are joined by a fleshy web only part of their length, as in the semipalmated plover.

When the fleshy webbing between the toes does not extend the entire length of the toe, it is called semipalmate, as in the semipalmated plover.

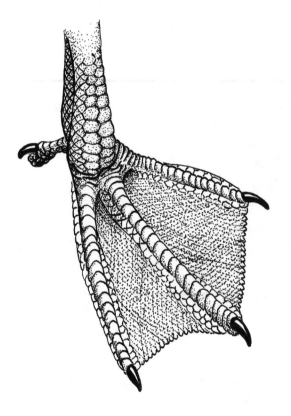

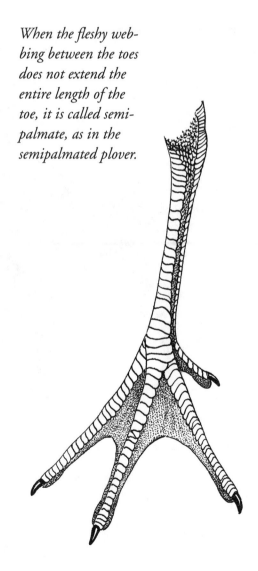

The palmate foot of a duck has fleshy webbing between the entire length of the three forward toes.

Totipalmate. All four toes are joined by ample webs, as in the cormorant and pelican.

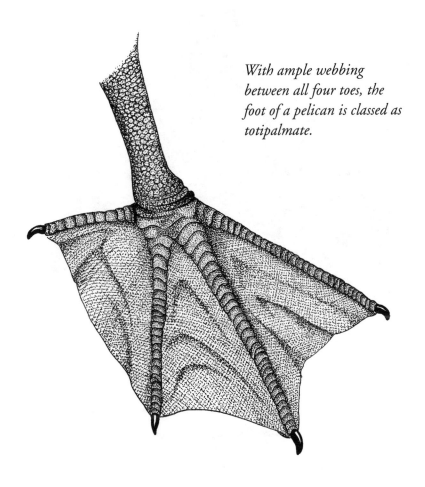

With ample webbing between all four toes, the foot of a pelican is classed as totipalmate.

Lobate. Toes have lateral lobes as in a grebe. Sometimes a foot is palmate with only the hallux being lobate, as in some diving ducks.

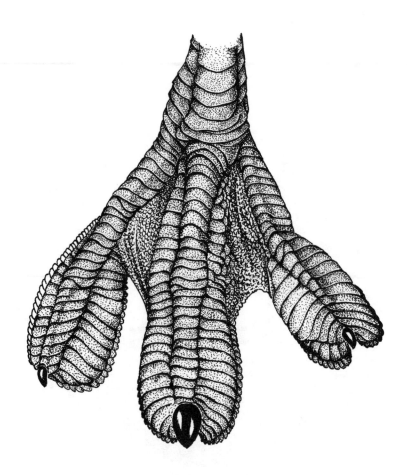

The grebe's foot has lobes growing along the sides of the toes and is called lobate.

TABLE II
Bird Families Classified by Toe Arrangement

Anisodactyl
(nearly all passerines)
buntings
creepers
crows
doves
finches
flycatchers
larks
nuthatches
sparrows

Heterodactyl
trogons

Lobate
coots
finfoots
grebes
phalaropes

Palmate
auks
ducks
flamingos
fulmars
geese
gulls
jaegers
loons
petrels
shearwaters
skimmers
swans

Pamprodactyl
colies
swifts

Raptorial
condors
eagles
falcons
hawks
kites
ospreys
vultures

Semipalmate
avocet
dotterel
greater yellowlegs
herons (two toes only)
semipalmated plover
semipalmated
    sandpiper
stilt sandpiper
upland plover
willet

Syndactyl
bee eaters
hoopoes
kingfishers
motmots
rollers
todys

Totipalmate
anhingas
boobies
cormorants
frigate birds
gannets
pelicans

Zygodactyl
barbets
cuckoos
honey guides
jacamars
owls
parakeets
parrots
toucans
woodpeckers
wrynecks

FIVE

Claws

Claws on a bird are a horny podotheca, or sheath, on the extreme phalanx of each toe. They provide protection for the tip of the toe and are well adapted for digging, scratching, preening, or fighting. Just like human toenails, the claw grows continuously, and it is worn down by abrasion from walking on hard surfaces, perching, scratching, or other uses. Claws are sometimes shed each spring and new ones grow in their place, as in the grouse.

The claws of a bird are generally curved, long, and sharply pointed. In birds of prey—hawks, eagles, owls—the claws are longer, thicker, curved, and sharp and are usually called talons. The acute nail, as in a woodpecker, is extremely curved and sharp whereas the obtuse nail, as in a grouse, is less curved and somewhat blunt. Lengthened nails are rather straight and elongated, as in some marsh birds like the jacana. These lengthened claws help to distribute the weight of the bird as it walks on the floating leaves of water plants.

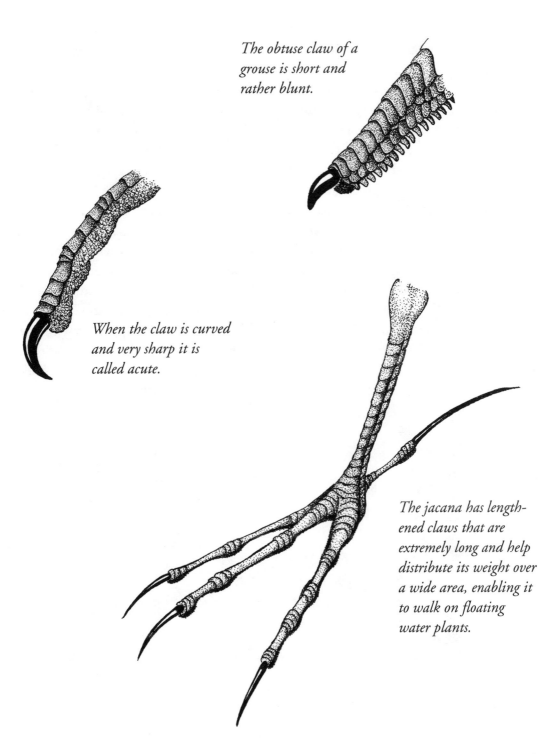

The obtuse claw of a grouse is short and rather blunt.

When the claw is curved and very sharp it is called acute.

The jacana has length-ened claws that are extremely long and help distribute its weight over a wide area, enabling it to walk on floating water plants.

In a few species the claw of the middle toe is pectinate. The inner edge of the claw has lateral scales like the teeth of a comb and is used for preening the head, neck, and bristles around the mouth. This feather comb clears the feathers and bristles of insects and parasites, as well as preening and straightening the feather barbs. Some species that have a pectinate middle claw are barn owls, herons, bitterns, and members of the nightjar family. The claws of a grebe are flattened, somewhat resembling a human fingernail, and are used as paddles for swimming.

As can be seen from the previous text and illustrations, there are literally hundreds of variations of feet. No two species have feet that are totally identical, and there may even be some variations in two birds of the same species that are of different sexes or ages.

Cast feet of many species are available from most suppliers of carving materials. These cast feet are very good references for studying the surface appearances of the various species, since the molds for the castings are made from the real feet.

Feet on a carving are frequently made of wood, wire, or epoxies. The methods of construction vary almost as greatly as the types of feet. Whatever method you choose for applying feet to your carving, the same basic rule applies as with any other part of the bird: Have good reference sources, take measurements, and know your anatomy.

The pectinate claw on the middle toe of a barn owl is sometimes referred to as the "feather comb" because its use creates the appearance of combing the feathers about the head.

FEATHER COMB

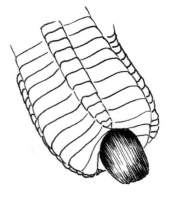

The grebe has a flattened claw that very much resembles a human fingernail.

SIX

Leg Muscles

Muscles are the motor mechanisms of all birds and animals. They are composed of bundles of sinuous fibers held together with a tissue sheath. The fibers taper at the ends, forming into tough, cordlike tendons that attach the muscles to the bone.

There are three types of muscles on a bird or animal: cardiac, smooth, and striated. Cardiac muscles are found only in the heart. Smooth muscles are found in blood vessels, glands, and in the skin at the base of the feathers. Striated muscles are usually associated with the skeleton and are the ones we are mainly concerned with here.

Muscle fibers are of two main types. One type includes twitch fibers and tonus fibers. The second type includes red fibers and white fibers. Nearly all muscles contain both red and white fibers, but the proportions vary depending on how a given muscle is used. Red fibers contain a richer supply of blood and do not fatigue easily, whereas the white fibers tire rapidly. The breast muscles of a migrating songbird contain mostly red fibers, but a grouse, which cannot fly for very long, has mostly white fibers in its breast muscles. These red and white fibers are also what give us the dark and light meat at Thanksgiving dinner.

A muscle can do work only by contraction or pulling (like a stretched rubber band). It cannot apply force by pushing. Therefore, for every muscle that causes a specific motion, there is usually a companion muscle that causes the opposite motion. Nearly all the striated muscles of the leg are paired to perform contradictory motions. The same muscles also appear on both the right side and the left side of the bird.

A bird has 175 different muscles with more than 2 dozen of them on the leg. Most of the leg muscles are located in the upper two-thirds of the leg. Only a few species such as hawks and owls, which grasp their prey with their toes, have well-developed muscles along the tarsus.

Surrounding the individual muscles are layers of tissue called fasciae, which keep the muscles separated and also act as a binder to hold them in position. A layer of tissue on the surface joins the skin to the muscle tissue. Tendons, which are the attachment devices that join the muscles to the bones, are found only at the extreme ends of each muscle.

The muscles of the leg are usually considered in two groups: the superficial muscles and the formula muscles. The artist or carver is concerned mainly with the superficial muscles as shown on page 43.

In the area of the femur (thigh), several muscles are attached at their dorsal end, with tendons, to the pelvic girdle and the vertebral column. These muscles create more than one-half of the bulk in the leg and mainly control the movement of the upper leg. Several more muscles lie in the area of the tibiotarsus and mainly control the movement of that part of the leg and of the foot.

Most people new to myology, the scientific study of the muscular system, are often discouraged by the long, Latin names of the muscles. Understanding the muscles is easier if you know how or why a muscle received its name. Often, the name is merely a compact description of the muscle itself or a single word describing the motion or action of the muscle, such as flexor or extensor. A flexor muscle causes the joint to bend, lessening the angle of the two bones, and an extensor muscle causes the joint to straighten. Flexor and extensor muscles work together but not at the same time. When one is relaxing, the other is contracting to produce movement.

Another way muscles are named is by their position or size in relation to other muscles in the same group: longus or brevis (long or short). Pairs of muscles, whose functions are similar, are named magnus and minimus (major and minor). Thus the extensor digitorium longus and the extensor digitorium brevis are a pair of muscles—one long and one short—that extends a digit or toe.

Sometimes a muscle is given a colorful

Most of the muscle mass on the leg of a bird is located on the upper two-thirds of the leg. Only a few species, such as hawks and owls, have well-developed muscles along the tarsus. There are more than two dozen muscles found in the leg of a bird.

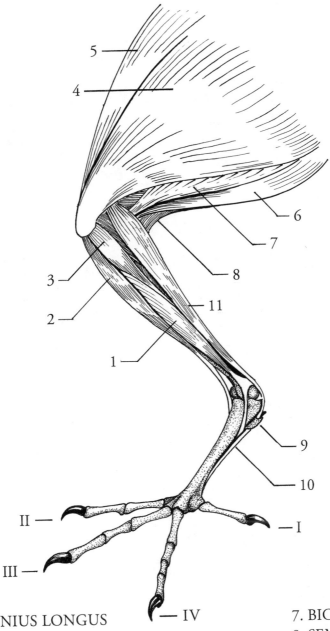

1. PERONIUS LONGUS
2. TIBIALIS ANTERIOR
3. FLEXOR PERFORANS
4. ILIOTIBIALIS
5. SARTORIUS
6. SEMITENDINOSUS

7. BICEPS FEMORIS
8. SEMIMEMBRANOSUS
9. HYPOTARSUS
10. TENDO-ACHILLES
11. GASTROCNEMIUS

or fancy name. The sartorius muscle, for example, is a long muscle that extends from the pelvis to the inner side of the tibiotarsus. The word *sartor* is Latin for tailor, and this is the muscle, in humans, that helps rotate the leg for sitting in tailor fashion with the legs crossed. A bird, of course, cannot cross its legs in tailor fashion, but the muscle is still named sartorius.

Nearly all the leg and foot muscles of a bird are located on the upper two-thirds of the leg. The muscles that control the foot and toes are also located in the area of the tibiotarsus. These muscles connect to the

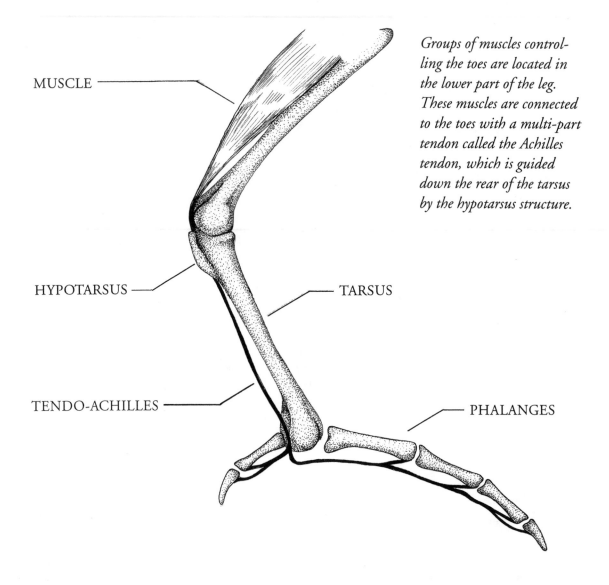

MUSCLE

HYPOTARSUS

TARSUS

TENDO-ACHILLES

PHALANGES

Groups of muscles controlling the toes are located in the lower part of the leg. These muscles are connected to the toes with a multi-part tendon called the Achilles tendon, which is guided down the rear of the tarsus by the hypotarsus structure.

toes with strong tendons and operate by a cable-and-pulley system to move the foot and toes.

At the rear of the tibiotarsus is a three-part muscle (gastrocnemius) that forms into a common tendon (tendo-achilles), which extends behind the heel. This tendon passes over the concave space between the ridges of the hypotarsus, which guides it down the rear of the tarsus, and is attached to the underside of the phalanges of the toes. This Achilles tendon, or flexor

tendon, along with the related muscle, is what causes the toes to clamp around an object when the bird is perching or grasping prey.

When the leg is drawn up close to the body, the Achilles tendon causes the toes to curl and grasp an object. This grasping action allows a bird to relax or sleep without falling off its perch. The Achilles tendon is relatively thick and prominent on the tarsus of most species.

When a bird squats on its perch, the Achilles tendon causes the toes to clamp around the perch, allowing the bird to rest or sleep without falling off.

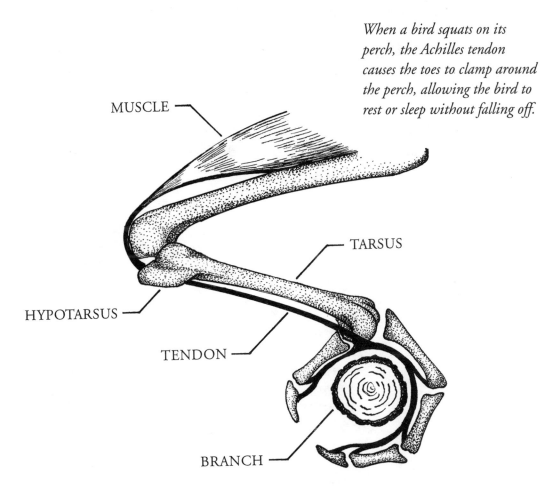

MUSCLE

TARSUS

HYPOTARSUS

TENDON

BRANCH

There are about thirty-five muscles in the leg of a bird, but not all species have the same number of leg muscles. Other than the primary or superficial muscles shown on page 43, there are eleven muscles known as formula muscles. These formula muscles are labeled by letter symbols, which makes a convenient method for ornithologists to record information. The "formula" for these eleven muscles is "A, B, C, D, E, F, G, X, Y, Am, and V."

Different species have a varied number of formula muscles. Instead of writing down the names of the formula muscles for a species, the ornithologist simply writes down the formula. A pigeon, for example, has ten of these muscles; the screech owl has only four, so the formula for a screech owl would be "A, D, E, G." The chimney swift has only two of the eleven formula muscles, so the formula would be "A, E."

The groups of muscles give the leg its mass and shape, although the amount of mass varies greatly among species. Generally, birds that spend a lot of time on the ground and little time flying usually will have heavier, better developed leg muscles. Examples of this would be the ruffed grouse, the turkey, and the ring-necked pheasant. These species have relatively large thighs and legs.

Knowing where the muscles are located and what they do can help you create more realistic positions for any bird you carve. Some of the master carvers prefer to make a clay model of their sculpture before even beginning the carving. With the clay sculpture they can easily change the size, shape, or position simply by adding or taking away clay. With this method you can experiment with the carving before you even begin cutting away any wood.

The eleven formula muscles are labeled A, B, C, D, E, F, G, X, Y, Am, and V. Not all species have the same number of these muscles. The screech owl has only four, but the chimney swift only has two.

A = Pars caudofemoralis

B = Pars iliofemoralis

C = Iliotrochantericus medius

D = Gluteus medius

E = Iliacus

F = Plantaris

G = Popliteus

X = Semitendinosus

Y = Accessory semitendinosus

Am = Ambiens

V = Vinculum

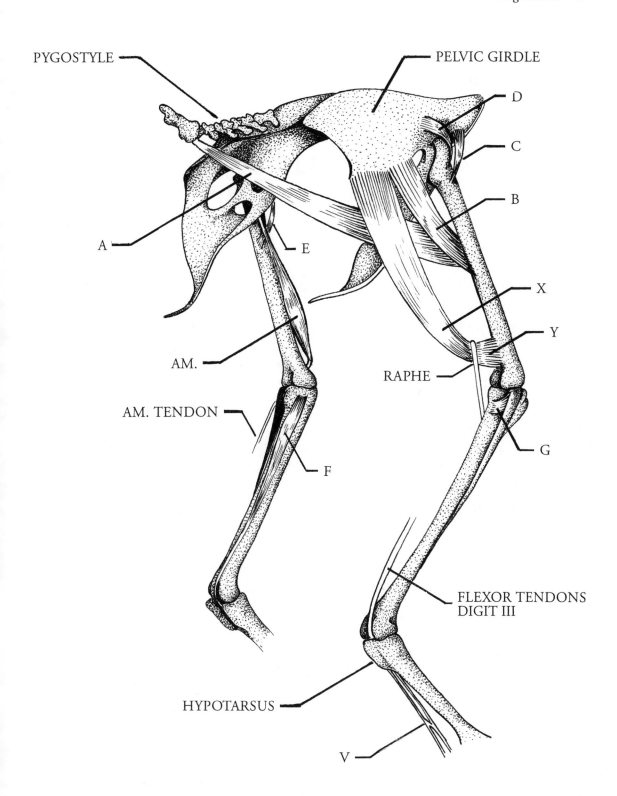

PYGOSTYLE

PELVIC GIRDLE

D

C

B

A

E

X

Y

AM.

RAPHE

AM. TENDON

G

F

FLEXOR TENDONS
DIGIT III

HYPOTARSUS

V

SEVEN

Covering

The skeletal-muscular system of all birds and animals have a covering known as the integument. In birds, this includes the skin, feathers, scales, claws, and bill.

The skin of a bird, compared with that of other animals, is quite thin yet it performs many functions. The primary function is, of course, to cover and protect the muscles and tissue that lie beneath it. The skin is made up of two layers. The outer layer or epidermis is very thin and contains cells that produce keratin, which is vital in the development of feathers and the scales of the horny podotheca of the tarsus and toes. Keratin is a protein material that in humans makes up the hair and fingernails.

The underlying layer, or dermis, of the skin is thicker than the epidermis and contains smooth muscles, nerves, and blood vessels. This fatty layer helps contain body heat, and the blood vessels give the bare skin the ability to change color, just as an embarrassed human would blush. This color change is sometimes quite apparent in the males of certain species during mating season. During courtship rituals the prairie chicken, for example, displays a bright, reddish gular region, and the male ring-necked pheasant has brilliant crimson cheek patches below the eyes.

The smooth muscles in the dermis are attached to the feather follicles and allow for movement of the feathers. The integument also contains oil glands used in preening, though not all species have these oil glands.

Another area of the integument is the fleshy soles on the bottoms of the toes, called the hypodactylum, but more commonly known as toe pads. All birds have toe pads, which generally have a roughened surface texture similar to coarse sandpaper. The toe pads tend to be thicker and fuller at the joints of the phalanges and less prominent between the joints. The integument that covers the toe pads is called the acropodium, and the rough surface texture of the acropodium helps the bird to better grip the surface upon which it is standing or walking. The surface of the acropodium is constantly being worn away by abrasion and is replenished by the keratin in the underlying fatty cells.

The size and thickness of the toe pads varies enormously among species. Birds of prey usually have very heavily padded toes, with a very rough acropodium, which aids them in holding on to their prey. These large wartlike scales of the acropodium are called tylari. The scales on the toe pads of the osprey's toes have small spines to help hold on to slippery fish.

The toe pads contain Herbst's corpuscles, which are found also in the bill, skin, and wings, and are very sensitive to vibration, thus increasing the sense of touch. Some ornithologists believe that these cor-

The toe pads of the osprey have wartlike scales called tylari that have protruding spines to help hold on to the slippery fish that constitute nearly all of their diet.

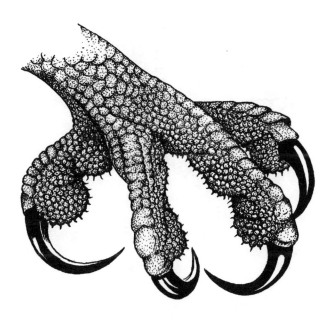

puscles are what signal a hawk's or an owl's foot to grasp shut the instant it touches the prey. This belief is further strengthened by the fact that Herbst's corpuscles appear in large amounts in the bills and mouths of birds that search for food with their bills. The skimmer, for example, will fly with its lower bill in the water and snap up small fish as it plows the water's surface in search of food. The high number of Herbst's corpuscles makes a skimmer's bill and mouth very sensitive to touch so that it can tell instantly when it is in contact with a fish.

Another peculiarity of the integument is found on the toes of the ruffed grouse. The grouse does not migrate, so during the winter months the toes grow a row of horny projections along each side. These "fringes" act like snowshoes and enable the grouse to better walk on the snow by distributing the weight over a wider area. These horny fringes are shed for the summer months when they are not needed. The ptarmigans accomplish the same effect with feathers on the toes that are shed in the summer.

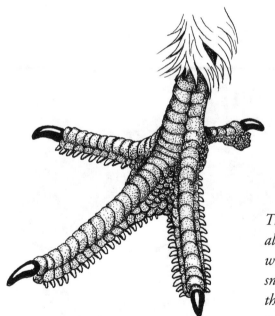

The ruffed grouse grows scaly fringes along the sides of its toes during the winter season. These fringes act like snowshoes and allow locomotion over the snow. They are shed for the summer season.

EIGHT

Plumage

The one characteristic that distinguishes birds from all other vertebrate animals is the presence of feathers. All birds grow feathers on most parts of their body, but feathers do not grow randomly in any area of a bird, including on the leg. The feathers on a bird are located in tracts and are arranged in a definite pattern within each tract.

There are two main feather tracts on the leg of a bird. The femoral tract is in the area of the femur, or thigh, and the crural tract is in the area of the crus.

The femoral tract is a narrow strip, on the distal side (outside) of the thigh, from the knee to a point rearward near the vent. The crural tract contains the remaining feathers of the leg. It begins at the knee and extends to the ankle, on both the inside and outside of the crus. There is a narrow apteria or bald spot at the knee between the femoral tract and the crural tract. The area where feathers grow within a tract is called a pteryla.

Generally, within any feather tract, the feathers grow in rows with each row offset slightly from the row above, not unlike the shingles on a roof. The angle and direction that the feathers grow, within a tract, are critical when carving or drawing a leg. The feathers in a tract remain in their relative position regardless of how the leg is positioned. For example, in the crural tract the feathers are aligned at an angle projecting downward and slightly rearward of the tibiotarsus. If the bird raises its leg to scratch its head, for instance, the feathers of the crural tract will still remain in the same position with respect to the tibiotarsus.

On all birds, the thigh is covered with plumage, as is all or part of the crus. Some birds have their tarsus totally or partially feathered, as in many owls, and some species have feathering over their toes, as in the Arctic grouse. When the tarsus or toes are feathered, these feathers nearly always lie parallel to that part of the appendage

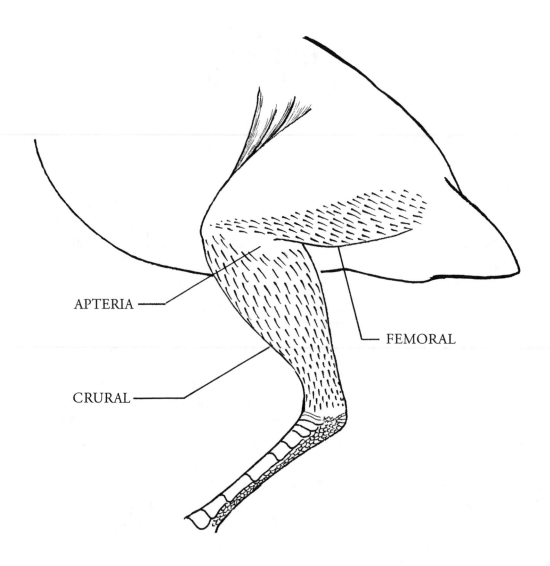

APTERIA

CRURAL

FEMORAL

The leg of a bird has two main feather tracts: the femoral and the crural. The bald space between feather tracts is called an apteria, and the feathered areas are called pterylae.

they are covering. These feathers of the tarsus and toes lie in what are sometimes termed the tarsal tract and the digital tract.

Feathers are what keep a bird warm, so it is only logical that the heavily muscled areas of the leg are where the feathers are located. Birds that have well-developed muscles along the tarsus, such as owls and hawks, also have feathers covering this area for warmth.

The skin of a bird, unlike the skin of humans, does not contain sweat glands. If a bird were to sweat, the feathers would soon become wet and useless for flight. In birds, the body temperature is controlled by a different process. The smooth muscles and nerves in the skin, which are attached to the feather follicles, allow the bird to move the feathers. They can be moved into either a raised, fluffed position or a flattened position. On a cold day, a bird will fluff its feathers, creating many air pockets that act as insulation to keep warm, and on a hot day it will flatten them close to the body, allowing body heat to dissipate faster.

When the tarsus and toes are feathered, as in many owls, these feathers lie in the tarsal tract and the digital tract, as seen on the great horned owl.

NINE

Position and Adaptation

With the exception of loons and grebes, birds walk on their toes, with their heels raised off the ground, and are said to be digitigrade, whereas humans are plantigrade and walk on their soles with their heels on the ground. A bird's method of locomotion on the ground, just as for a human, is called bipedalism, which means that the body is mostly upright and the two hind limbs are used for walking. However, not all birds walk in the same manner or style. The stride by which a certain species walks is largely dependent upon the length of the femur relative to the tibiotarsus.

Ground-dwelling birds, such as the grouse and the wild turkey, generally have strong legs with relatively long femurs that enable them to walk or run smoothly. Nearly all birds that walk can also run, but some species run better and faster than others. The ostrich is a typical running bird and can attain speeds of 40–50 miles per hour, covering 12 feet or more with each stride. The roadrunner has been clocked at 15 mph and can outrun humans. Most shorebirds also run quite well.

Some birds will hop, with both feet together, rather than walk, as is seen in catbirds, nuthatches, and wrens. Hopping is generally more tiring than walking since the weight of the entire body must be raised with each hop. All species that hop can also walk and most that walk can also run.

Birds use their legs and feet for much more than simply perching on a branch, walking, running, or hopping. Ground feeding birds such as the towhee, sparrow, and junco also use their feet to scratch the ground in search of food. These birds will often hop forward, then backward, using both feet on the backward hop to move leaves or debris that may be covering food. This behavior is called the "double scratch."

The one-footed scratch is common in the domestic chicken, grouse, quail, and wild turkey.

Different species use their legs and feet for different purposes. The talons and toes of a hawk or an owl become a lethal weapon when catching prey. Feet are used by most birds to scratch and preen themselves, and some species are known to use their feet and legs to carry their young chicks to a safer nesting site. Many birds use their feet, along with their bills, to turn their eggs during incubation. The webbed or lobated feet of waterfowl become propellers when these birds are swimming and water skis when they are landing on water.

When a duck is swimming, its foot is perfectly suited as a paddle. As the foot moves forward in the water, the toes are held close together and the webbing relaxes between the toes. This creates a relatively small area with little resistance to the water. On the power stroke, the toes are spread wide and the webbing is stretched to form a broad paddle that pushes the duck forward in the water. All ducks swim by alternating leg positions; when one leg is forward, the other is to the rear.

Grebes use their lobed feet for swimming in a slightly different fashion. The lobes are rigidly attached to the toes. On the return stroke, the foot is rotated nearly ninety degrees so that the inner side lobe is pointed forward and "cuts" through the water like a knife. On the power stroke, the foot is returned to the normal position and the lobes act like a paddle. In other lobed species, the lobes are less rigid and simply fold back during the return stroke.

When a duck walks on land, it has quite an awkward manner of locomotion. This characteristic "waddle" stems from the fact that the femur is considerably shorter than the tibiotarsus, and the pelvic girdle is rather narrow when compared with other birds. The femur, being short, is positioned almost horizontal to the ground so that the feet are placed under the center of gravity. The mechanics of this arrangement are well suited for swimming but not for walking, since the tarsi and feet are angled slightly inward to support the weight. As a duck takes a step, it must shift all the body weight to the foot on the ground, and the striding foot swings in a slightly outward arc as it moves forward. This alternating weight shifting and arcing stride causes a swing or waddle when the bird is walking.

It is not certain whether the shapes of the leg and foot determine the habits of the bird or if the habits of the bird have been the determining factors in the evolution of its leg and foot shape. Did the heron develop long legs because it is a wader, or does it wade in search of food because it has long legs? In any case, all birds are physically well adapted to deal with their habitat and lifestyles.

A bird's foot is practically void of fleshy muscle and nerves and has very little blood flow. When the tarsus has muscle it is usually covered with plumage for warmth, as in most owls. The foot is nearly immune to extreme temperatures—hot or cold. Occasionally, a bird's toes will freeze in winter, but this seems to be the exception. When perching, a bird often has its feet drawn up into the belly feathers, which gives the feet protection from the cold.

The feet of a bird are, to some extent, kept warm by their unique system of blood vessels. The arteries, which supply warm blood to the feet, are divided into several smaller branches that are intertwined with the branched veins that return the cooler blood. The warmer arteries tend to reheat the blood in the veins, thus maintaining an even temperature in the foot. This natural "heat recovery system" is quite prevalent in ducks and geese and allows them to stand on ice or swim in icy waters without freezing their feet.

The feet of a bird are not immune, however, to disease, and many birds will contract a virus known as "avian pox," "foot pox," or "avian diphtheria." This disease is confined to birds and does not affect man or other animals. Symptoms of the avian pox are the growth of wartlike spots on the feet with a mild infection.

Leg position is very important to the wildfowl artist, but it is often overlooked or misunderstood. A perfectly good carving is often poorly displayed because of inaccurate leg positions. Legs have a definite "set" or attitude that varies among species and depending on what the bird is doing.

When in flight, most perching birds draw their legs up close to the body. This position helps to streamline their shape, thus making it easier to fly. Sometimes the feet are totally hidden under the feathers of the flank and abdomen. Birds with longer tarsi simply extend their legs to the rear and tuck them under the tail. Only a few birds will let their legs dangle downward while flying, as is sometimes seen in the woodcock.

The positions of the legs and feet are dependent upon many factors. The skeletal sizes of different species vary greatly and have a great influence on leg position. A bird that spends a lot of its time walking usually has a wider pelvic region and a relatively long femur. This distributes the center of gravity over a wider area, and the longer femur sets the feet farther forward, causing the bird to stand more erect, which makes walking smoother and steadier. Many waterfowl, such as grebes, which spend most of their lifetime in water, have a proportionately shorter femur and a narrower pelvic region. This gives the appearance that the legs are attached more to the rear of the body, and in a few cases this is

true, as in the loon. This arrangement
streamlines the body for swimming but is
a handicap to the bird when walking.
Some waterfowl spend nearly all their life
in the water and have a very difficult time
walking on land.

*The leg muscles of a loon are such that
the leg appears to be located well to the
rear of the body. This arrangement is
suitable for swimming but is a great
handicap for walking.*

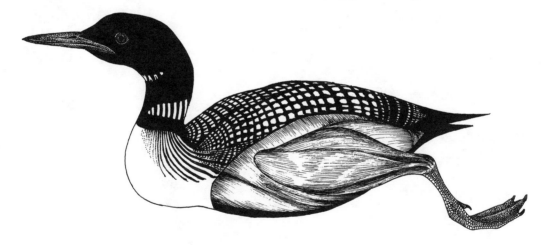

Sometimes a bird will stand on just one foot, usually for the purpose of resting. During this one-legged stance, the body weight is shifted so that the center of gravity is over the one leg. To the casual observer, this makes the tarsus appear to be attached to the underside of the bird. If the weight were not shifted to the support leg, the bird would fall over. Many carvers fail to show the shifted weight when they carve a bird that is standing in this position.

When a bird rests with one leg raised, the body weight is shifted so that the foot is located at the center of gravity almost at the middle of the belly.

Some species have the awkward appearance of being knock-kneed. The heels are placed well under the body and the feet are spread apart for balance. The barn owl and burrowing owl are good examples of this posture.

With the heels placed well under the body and the feet spread wide apart, the burrowing owl has a knock-kneed stance.

Legs and feet are also used as shock absorbers when a bird alights on a perch. As the bird approaches a branch, the legs are extended to grasp the perch. The extended legs absorb some of the impact, thus making it a soft landing. The webbed feet of waterfowl serve the same purpose when the birds land on water. The feet absorb the impact against the water and become a pair of water skis to slow down forward motion.

When a bird is about to alight on a branch, the legs are extended and help absorb some of the shock.

The webbed feet of a duck become a pair of water skis, absorbing the impact when the duck lands on the water and slows down forward motion.

What color is the bird's foot? This question poses a sometimes difficult problem for the carver or artist. Located in the skin, feathers, bills, and feet of birds are pigments called carotenoids that are responsible for all the colors of the bird including the feet. Carotenoids were named from the pigment in the root of the ordinary carrot.

Colors can be described in so many different ways that a verbal description is almost useless to the artist. Each paint manufacturer, for reasons of patent or copyright protection, has its own names for its pigments. Not being familiar with paint color names, an ornithologist or naturalist might describe the foot as being "slate" or "dark-sandy" colored.

We know that slate has many different colors, and you would not paint the feet of a robin the color of green or red slate. Color photographs can be a good reference, but because of light diffraction, the camera sees color somewhat differently than the human eye. Also, the chemical processing for film varies so that not all photos are accurate examples of the true color.

Nor can you depend on a taxidermy mount for color reference. The taxidermist must also paint the feet of his specimens because the color of the horny podotheca begins to fade and disappear immediately after the bird's death. On many species the color of the foot will vary, sometimes drastically, with the season or with the habitat and diet.

Some of the dabbling ducks, for instance, will have dark-colored feet (black or brown) while they are living and feeding in the tidewater marshes of the Atlantic coast. After they have migrated inland to fresh water and changed their diet, their feet turn a much lighter color (yellow or orange). This color change corresponds with the mating season when the plumage also becomes more colorful and brilliant.

Whatever the cause, there are color changes in the feet of some species throughout the year, and a thorough study of the species is necessary before painting your carving or illustration. Your best reference is a pair of binoculars and many trips to the field, zoo, or aviary to make written and mental notes.

TEN

Special Adaptations

A bird is a highly specialized vertebrate, and the two areas that are perhaps the most specialized are the bill and the feet. Throughout the millennia birds' feet have evolved to adapt to the necessary requirements of the species and the habitat. The webbed or lobed feet of most water birds are ideal for swimming; the acute claws of tree climbing birds such as the woodpecker are extremely curved and sharp; and the heavily padded, powerful feet of the raptors are excellent weapons for subduing their prey.

Some species of shorebirds have semi-palmate feet, which enable them to walk on the soft muddy base of shallow waters. The jacana has extremely long toes and claws that allow it to walk on floating water plants, thus enabling it to reach a safe haven where animal predators cannot, or will not, venture. The wild turkey uses its strong, well-developed legs and feet to scratch the ground in search of food and to build a nest for incubation.

When the osprey transports a captured fish to its nest, it will nearly always hold the fish with both feet, aligning the head to the front. This streamlines the fish aerodynamically and makes flying easier, thus consuming less energy.

Nearly all birds use their feet to scratch or preen themselves, and members of the parrot family use their feet like hands to eat. In winter, grouse grow digital feathers or fringes on their toes, which work like snowshoes, and the pectinate claw of some herons and nightjars enable them to clean the feathers about the head.

Feet are also used extensively during courtship rituals. The male sage grouse does a tantalizing two-step to impress the female during his courtship display. The bald eagle nuptial pair will lock toes in flight while one of the pair flies upside down. This practice is not unlike the holding of hands by humans in a display of affection.

Although the above-mentioned adaptations are somewhat generalized, there are a few species whose legs and feet have evolved to a more specialized form. The loon, for example, has a markedly different skeleto-muscular system than other species have.

Loons are not digitigrade, as are most other birds, and tend to walk on the entire foot with the heel on the ground. There are several reasons for this plantigrade locomotion. The pelvis of a loon is relatively narrow and projects farther rearward than that of most other species. This makes the attachment point of the femur more to the rear of the bird. Also, the tibiotarsus is much longer than the femur, which puts the heel far back on the bird and does not allow the feet to be under the center of gravity. In order to walk, the loon must raise its body nearly vertically upright for balance, and it is easier for it to walk with the heel on the ground.

The muscular system of a loon's leg is also unique in that the muscles of the thigh and crus are more compact and located close to the body. This arrangement restricts upper leg movement and greatly hinders walking. This position is an asset though for swimming because the means of propulsion are located at the rear like the propeller on a motorboat. Penguins have a similar arrangement but do not use their feet as a propeller. Penguins swim mainly with their wings, using them as flippers much like a seal.

Except for, perhaps, the various colors of birds, legs and feet have more characteristic differences than any other part of the anatomy. These differences help the ornithologist place a species in the proper class, order, family, or subfamily and also provide information about sex and age differences. Characteristics of the feet can tell us much about the habits of a species when little else is known about a particular bird. With the modern techniques of X ray and ultrasound, the development of legs and feet can be studied from the embryonic stage through adulthood without destroying the egg or the bird.

ELEVEN

Measurement

When cataloging a species, an ornithologist will take many measurements. Accurate measurements are taken for several reasons. They help identify the differences between sexes of a species, and they determine the rate of growth in young birds. Unfortunately, there is no formula to determine the leg size of a bird. You cannot assume that the middle toe will be half the length of the tarsus (even though this is true in many species)

or that the tarsus and tibiotarsus are of equal length. There appears to be, however, a general relationship of leg size to length of the neck. When the legs are rather long, so is the neck.

There is no mathematical method to calculate the size of a leg. The only sure way to be accurate about the size of the leg is to measure. These measurements, when available, can be quite useful to the carver or artist.

The tarsus measurement (Tar.) is taken from the ankle joint to the lower edge of the last scutellum (point where the middle toe is attached) and always on the anterior or front side of the tarsus. The middle toe (number III) is normally the longest and is measured from the point where it attaches at the tarsus to the end of the last phalanx, not including the claw.

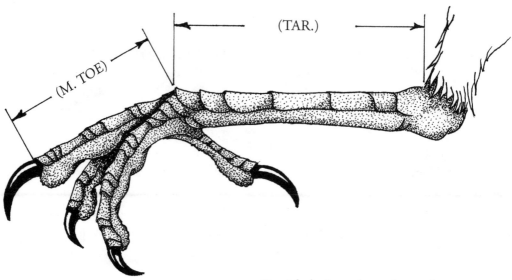

Ornithologists take and record measurements to determine differences in sex or age. On charts, the tarsus measurement is identified as "Tar.," and the middle toe as "M. Toe." Dimensions are generally recorded in millimeters, but some charts also show the dimensions in inches.

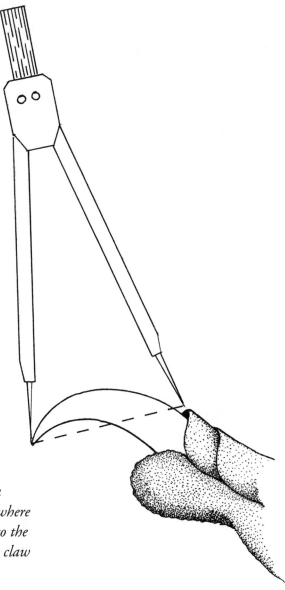

The claws are measured in a straight line from the point where the claw attaches at the toe to the extreme tip, even though the claw may be curved.

Many natural history museums have collections of bird study skins. The Museum of Natural History in New York City has the largest collection with more than 900,000 study skins. With a few phone calls, you can usually arrange to have access to specimens from these collections so that you can make notes, take measurements, photograph, and become familiar with the species you want to carve. These study skins are an invaluable aid to the carver or artist.

Measurements are usually taken and recorded in millimeters by ornithologists. For your convenience, a conversion chart is included on page 69.

TABLE III
Measurement Conversion

FRACTION	DECIMAL	MM	FRACTION	DECIMAL	MM
1/64	.01562	.397	33/64	.51562	13.097
1/32	.03125	.794	17/32	.53125	13.494
3/64	.04688	1.191	35/64	.54688	13.891
1/16	.06250	1.588	9/16	.56250	14.288
5/64	.07812	1.984	37/64	.57812	14.684
3/32	.09375	2.381	19/32	.59375	15.081
7/64	.10938	2.778	39/64	.60938	15.478
1/8	.12500	3.175	5/8	.62500	15.875
9/64	.14062	3.572	41/64	.64062	16.272
5/32	.15625	3.969	21/32	.65625	16.669
11/64	.17188	4.366	43/64	.67188	17.066
3/16	.18750	4.763	11/16	.68750	17.463
13/64	.20312	5.159	45/64	.70312	17.859
7/32	.21875	5.556	23/32	.71875	18.256
15/64	.23438	5.953	47/64	.73438	18.653
1/4	.25000	6.350	3/4	.75000	19.050
17/64	.26562	6.747	49/64	.76562	19.447
9/32	.28125	7.144	25/32	.78125	19.844
19/64	.29688	7.541	51/64	.79688	20.241
5/16	.31250	7.938	13/16	.81250	20.638
21/64	.32812	8.334	53/64	.82812	21.034
11/32	.34375	8.731	27/32	.84375	21.431
23/64	.35938	9.128	55/64	.85938	21.828
3/8	.37500	9.525	7/8	.87500	22.225
25/64	.39062	9.922	57/64	.89062	22.622
13/32	.40625	10.319	29/32	.90625	23.019
27/64	.42188	10.716	59/64	.92188	23.416
7/16	.43750	11.113	15/16	.93750	23.813
29/64	.45312	11.509	61/64	.95312	24.209
15/32	.46875	11.906	31/32	.96875	24.606
31/64	.48438	12.303	63/64	.98438	25.003
1/2	.50000	12.700	1	1.00000	25.4

TWELVE

Learning More

For millions of years, man has been infatuated with birds. In recent times the quest for knowledge has led man into areas of intensive study of these feathered creatures. Most of what is known about birds today has been compiled from lifetimes of studies by ornithologists.

The carver or artist will probably not devote a lifetime to the scientific studies of birds, but a good working knowledge of the anatomy and muscular system will help in producing more accurate renderings. Books are a good source for learning, but the hands-on approach may be more beneficial than reading a book. The actual dissection of a bird is invaluable to the learning experience. This is not to imply that a bird should sacrifice its life just to further your knowledge. Not only is it illegal to kill or take a wild bird without a special permit, the killing of any wild bird is a senseless waste.

A chicken, duck, or turkey purchased at the local supermarket will suffice as a specimen. Usually, at oriental markets, you can find chickens or ducks with the feet still intact. With one of these specimens you can proceed to examine and dissect the leg to see the actual skin, muscle, and bone structure.

Look first at the skin to see the "pimples" of the feather follicles and where the feather tracts are located, then remove the skin and study the muscles. Flex the joints and note the action of each leg segment. Removal of the muscles will expose the bones for further observation. If the muscles are carefully removed, the ligaments are readily visible.

The best part of this project is that when you have finished dissecting your specimen, the parts can be placed in a pot of boiling water, along with some spices, and converted into a delicious bowl of soup.

Self Test

1. The three main segments of the leg are _____, _____, and _____.

2. The knee of a bird bends in what direction?

3. The part that most people mistake for the leg is actually the _____.

4. There are normally two main feather tracts on the leg. They are the _____ and _____.

5. The skin, feathers, and scales that cover a bird are called the _____.

6. The part of the integument that covers the tarsus with a horny surface is called the _____.

7. A foot with heavy toe pads and long, sharp claws is classed as _____.

8. A palmated foot has webbing between which toes?

9. When the webbing does not extend the full length of the toes it is classed as _____.

10. A tarsus covered with overlapping plates is called_____.

11. What are the three main cross-section shapes of a tarsus?

12. Another name for a pectinate claw is _____.

13. A tarsus covered with irregular horny plates is called _____.

14. When the hallux is attached higher than the other toes it is said to be

_____.

15. Spurs grow on what part of the leg?

16. A featherless area of the skin is called _____.

17. The feathered areas of the skin are called _____.

18. The larger of the two bones in the lower part of the leg is the _____.

19. The bones of the toes are called _____.

20. How many phalanges does toe number III have? _____ Number II ? _____

21. The femur is in which segment?

22. Another name for the tarsus is the _____.

23. The crus is commonly called the _____.

24. Carotenoids are what give _____to the feet.

25. Walking on the toes, with the heel raised, is called _____.

Answers on page 80

Glossary

Acetabulum. The socket of the pelvic girdle that receives the head of the femur.

Achilles tendon. The heavy, multipart tendon, at the rear of the tarsus, that attaches the flexor muscles to the toes.

Acropodium. The podotheca that covers the bottoms of the toes.

Acrotarsium. The part of the podotheca that covers the front surface of the tarsus.

Acute. A type of claw shape, being curved, long, and sharply pointed.

Acutiplantar. Having the rear of the tarsus form a sharp ridge.

Anatomy. The scientific study of the internal structure of a bird or animal, including the skeletal, muscular, neural, vascular, reproductive, and digestive systems. Anatomy is usually accomplished by dissection.

Anisodactyl. The most common arrangement of a bird's toes, in which the hallux is pointed to the rear and the remaining three toes are pointed forward.

Anterior. Referring to the frontal portion of a particular part or area of the anatomy, as opposed to posterior.

Apteria. The featherless or bald areas on the skin of a bird.

Archeopteryx. Name given to a prehistoric bird of about 150 million years ago. Its fossil remains were unearthed in 1861 in Bavaria.

Articulated joint. A movable joint of the skeleton.

Bipedalism. A form of locomotion in birds and animals in which the body is raised upright and supported by the two hind limbs, as in humans.

Booted. The surface appearance of the tarsus being smooth, without scales; ocreate.

Cannon bone. A name given to the tarsometatarsus bone because its shape resembles the barrel of a gun.

Cardiac muscle. Muscle found only in the heart.

Carotenoids. Color pigments found in the feathers, skin, bills, and feet of birds.

Claw. The horny extremity of the last phalanx of the toe; see also TALON.

Cnemial crest. The enlarged portion of the tibiotarsus at the dorsal (upper) end, on the frontal side.

Compressed. A shape of the tarsus that in cross-section is flattened side to side with sharp ridges front and back.

Crural. Pertaining to the crus or tibiotarsus.

Crural tract. A feather tract of the leg located between the knee and ankle.

Crus. The segment of the leg from the knee to the ankle joint.

Dermis. The secondary layer of the skin; see also EPIDERMIS.

Digital formula. A method in ornithology using Roman numerals to label the toes; the hallux is always toe number I.

Digitigrade. Walks or stands on the toes with the heel raised off the ground.

Digits. A term referring to the toes individually.

Distal. A term used in anatomy to describe the point farthest from the centerline of the body. This term is often used when describing parts of the foot; e.g., the distal end of the femur (opp.—proximal).

Dorsal. A term used to refer to the top part, or top view, of a bird or animal (opp.—ventral).

Elevated hallux. A hallux that is attached higher up on the tarsus than are the other toes, so that it does not fully touch the ground in normal stance, as in the ring-necked pheasant.

Epidermis. The outermost layer of the skin.

Extensor. Any muscle that extends or straightens a joint.

Fascia. A sheet of connective tissue that envelops a muscle or other part of the body. Fasciae also join the skin to the body (pl. fasciae).

Feather comb. Name given to the pectinate middle claw of some species because it is used to comb the feathers to rid them of dirt and parasites.

Feather follicle. A cavity or depression in the skin from which a feather grows.

Feather tract. An area of a bird from which a particular group of feathers grows, such as the femoral tract.

Femur. The uppermost bone of the leg (thigh) attached, at the proximal end, to the pelvic girdle.

Femoral. Referring to the area of the femur, as in femoral tract.

Femoral tract. A feather tract located on the upper (proximal) segment of the leg.

Fibula. An incomplete bone of the lower leg, lying parallel to, and almost never as long as, the tibiotarsus.

Flattened. A type of claw shape resembling the nails of a human, as in the grebe.

Flexor. Any muscle that bends or reduces the angle of a joint.

Foot. The lower extremity of the leg, made up of the toes, claws, and tarsus. Generally the foot is mistakenly thought of as only the toes and claws.

Formula muscles. A specific group of eleven muscles of the leg that are identified by letters of the alphabet. The number of formula muscles varies among species.

Hallux. The number I toe of a bird, having two phalanges and usually pointing rearward (pl. hallus).

Heel. Anatomically, the enlarged upper end of the tarsus at the rear.

Herbst's corpuscles. Found primarily in the bills and feet of birds, these corpuscles are believed to make these parts sensitive to touch.

Heterodactyl. Having the number I and number II toes turned to the rear, as in trogons.

Hind toe. See HALLUX.

Holothecal. A term referring to a smooth podotheca of the tarsus; booted.

Homologous. Structurally similar to, as the leg of a bird is homologous to the leg of man.

Hypodactylum. The sole of the toes; toe pad.

Hypotarsus. A bone structure on the rear of the tarsus, having two or more ridges, that forms a guide for the Achilles tendon.

Incumbent. A hallux that is joined to the tarsus at the same level as the number II, III, and IV toes.

Integument. The outer covering of a bird or animal, including the skin, scales, claws, and bill.

Joint. The point where two bones meet. There are two types of joints: suture and articulated.

Keratin. Found in the integument of a bird, this compound is used for the formation of feathers and the horny growth of the podotheca.

Latiplantar. Having the rear of the tarsus rounded.

Leg. Anatomically, the segments of the femur and the tibiotarsus; the area between the pelvis and the ankle of the hind limb.

Lengthened. The shape of a claw being extremely long, as in the jacana.

Ligament. A strong cordlike tissue that binds bones together at joints.

Lobate. Having lateral lobes along the sides of toes, as in the grebe.

Metatarsus. See TARSOMETATARSUS.

Middle toe. Toe number III in the digital formula, having four phalanges.

Morphology. The scientific study of the visible surface areas of a bird or animal.

Myology. The scientific study of the muscular system of birds or animals.

Obtuse. A claw shape that is rather short and blunt.

Ocreate. The surface appearance of the tarsus being smooth, without scales; booted.

Ornithology. The scientific overall study of birds, including their shape, size, color, functions, traits, and habits.

Osteology. The scientific study of bones and the skeletal system of birds and animals.

Palmated. A foot type in which the three forward toes (numbers II, III, IV) are joined by a fleshy web, as in most ducks and geese.

Pamprodactyl. All four toes of the foot are turned forward, as in the swift.

Patella. A small bone at the anterior (frontal side) of the knee. Not all species have a patella.

Pectinate. Term used when the claw of the middle toe has toothlike projections along the side, as in the whippoorwill and the barn owl.

Pelvic girdle. The skeletal structure that provides a socket for the femur. It is made up of the ilium, ischium, and pubis, which are joined together to form a platelike support; the hip of the bird.

Phalanges. All the bones of the toes; one of the bones is a phalanx.

Planta. The posterior surface of the tarsus from the heel to the toes; the sole of the foot.

Plantigrade. Walks on the sole of the foot with the heel on the ground.

Plumage. All the feathers of a bird, collectively.

Podotheca. The scaly, horny integument of the tarsus and toes.

Posterior. Referring to the rear or hind portion in anatomy.

Preening. The act of smoothing the feathers and caring for them to remove dirt, oil, and parasites.

Proximal. In anatomy, a term used to describe the point closest to the centerline of the body, as the proximal end of the femur (opp.—distal).

Pterna. The pad on the heel.

Pterylae. Areas of the skin where feathers grow (opp.—apteria).

Raptorial. A type of foot in which the toes are heavily padded and the claws are long, curved, and sharply pointed, as in eagles, hawks, and owls.

Reticulate. The surface of the tarsus being covered with small irregular plates.

Scutellate. The surface of the tarsus being covered with overlapping plates or scales, as in the grosbeak.

Scutella. The name for the horny plates that cover the tarsus and toes.

Semipalmate. A type of foot in which the forward-pointing toes are joined for only part of their length by a fleshy web, as in the semipalmated plover.

Serrate. Toothed, like a saw.

Shank. Another name for the tarsus.

Spurred. A type of foot that has an outgrowth on the tarsus, at the inner rear, that creates a spur, as in the ring-necked pheasant.

Striated. Stringy or marked with streaks, as in striated muscles.

Suture. The name given to a joint of two bones that do not articulate or move with respect to each other.

Syndactyl. A type of foot that has two or more toes that are joined for part of their length and that share a common sole, as in the belted kingfisher.

Synovial. A type of articulated joint that is encapsulated and filled with a lubricant called synovial fluid.

Talon. The claw on a bird of prey, generally longer, sharper, and more curved than claws on other birds.

Tarsal sheath. See PODOTHECA.

Tarsal tract. A feather tract found on some species, which is in the area of the tarsus and includes the toes, as in owls.

Tarsometatarsus. Generally referred to as the tarsus or metatarsus; this is what most people call the "leg," but it is actually the upper part of the foot.

Tarsus. See TARSOMETATARSUS.

Tendons. Strong sinuous fibers that attach the muscles to the bones.

Tibiotarsus. The main, lower leg bone of a bird; located between the tarsus and the femur, it is comparable to the tibia of a human; crus.

Topography. In ornithology, a term referring to a "map" of the visible surface of a bird in order to define areas.

Totipalmate. A type of foot having all four toes connected by a fleshy web of skin, as in pelicans.

Tract. See FEATHER TRACT.

Tylari. The rough pads on the bottom surface of the toes.

Ventral. Pertaining to the underside or the bottom view; in the area of the vent, as the ventral view of the tail.

Vertebral column. The bones constituting the spine or backbone of a bird or animal.

Zygodactyl. A foot type having two toes pointing forward and two pointing rearward, as in woodpeckers.

Bibliography

Although a great number of sources were used as reference material for this book, the primary sources were as follows:

Brooke, M., and T. Birkhead, eds. *Cambridge Encyclopedia of Ornithology*. New York: Cambridge Press, 1991.

Burne, David. *Bird*. Eyewitness Books. London: Dorling Kindersly Ltd., 1988.

Farner, D. S., J. R. King, Jr., and K. C. Parkes, eds. *Avian Biology*. 2 vols. New York: Academic Press, 1971.

Pasquier, Roger R. *Watching Birds: An Introduction to Ornithology*. Boston: Houghton Mifflin Co., 1977.

Peterson, Roger Tory. *The Birds*. Life Nature Library. New York: Time Inc., 1963.

Pettingill, O. S., Jr. *Ornithology in Laboratory and Field*. Orlando: Academic Press, 1985.

Terres, J. K. *Encyclopedia of North American Birds*. New York: Wings Books, 1991.

VanTyne, J., and A. J. Berger. *Fundamentals of Ornithology*. New York: Dover Publications, 1971.

TEST ANSWERS

1. femoral (thigh), crus (drumstick), foot (tarsus and toes)

2. forward

3. tarsus (shank) or upper part of the foot

4. femoral and crural

5. integument

6. podotheca

7. raptorial

8. the three forward toes

9. semipalmate

10. scutellate

11. rounded in front, rounded front and back, and compressed

12. feather comb

13. reticulate

14. elevated

15. inner rear of the tarsus

16. apteria

17. pterylae

18. tibiotarsus (tibia)

19. phalanges

20. 4, 3

21. femoral

22. shank, metatarsus, or tarsometatarsus

23. drumstick

24. color

25. digitigrade

ABOUT THE AUTHOR

Jack Kochan is a veteran bird carver whose interest in the hobby was sparked ten years ago by a visit to a decoy factory. Since then his carvings have earned numerous awards, including first-place honors at the Ward World Championships in 1990. He credits his success to his knowledge of avian anatomy, which he says helps him create detailed, lifelike carvings. As an artist and illustrator, Kochan has produced work for a variety of publications. An avid outdoorsman, he lives in Leesport, Pennsylvania.

The Bird Carving Basics Series
by Curtis J. Badger

This series offers world-class carving tips at a reasonable price. Each volume presents a variety of techniques from carvers like Jim Sprankle, Leo Osborne, Martin Gates, and Floyd Scholz. Illustrated with exceptional step-by-step photos.

The eleven volume series:

Eyes

Feet

Habitat

Tools

Heads

Bills and Beaks

Texturing

Painting

Special Painting Techniques

Songbird Painting

How to Compete

For complete ordering information, write:

STACKPOLE
BOOKS

5067 Ritter Road
Mechanicsburg, PA 17055
or call 1-800-732-3669